Financial Analysis Of a Divorce

How a CDFA® can help with your family law practice.

Natalie Grignon, CDFA®, CIM®

Also by Natalie Grignon:

Wealth 101 for Teenagers

ISBN: 978-1-9994684-0-8

Richesse pour ados

ISBN: 978-1-9994684-2-2

Dedication

To my children; being a mother made me want to be a good person for myself, for you and for my community.

To all of you whom I have met,

Whether you are currently part of my life or have been in the past; you helped shaped my life.

I am blessed & grateful.

ISBN: 978-1-9994684-4-6

© 2019 Natalie Grignon

Although the author has made every effort to ensure that the information in this book was correct at press time, the author does not assume and hereby disclaim any liability to any party for any loss, damage, or disruption caused by errors or omissions, whether such errors or omissions result from negligence, accident, or any other cause. The information in this book is meant to supplement, not replace, legal, accounting, or professional advice.

The usage of the term **CDFA®** has been used instead of **CDFA® professional** (the short-form has been used throughout the book to ease the reading)

Book design by: BT Covers
Author Photograph by: Chantale Arsenault

Contents

Introduction

Chapters:

1) The Institute for Divorce Financial Analysts™, and its certification
2) How a CDFA® contributes in your divorce cases
3) What a CDFA® Professional cannot do
4) Delegate the financial analysis tasks to grow your practice.
5) For mediators; how a CDFA® can help with the negotiations
6) Effectively use a CDFA® as an Expert witness
7) Find a CDFA® that matches your firm's vision.

Introduction

In your family law practice, you might be confronted with situations where your financial knowledge will be put to the test.

Most of your cases will involve a small list of assets of a house and a few investment accounts. However, in those cases where there is significant wealth and financial documents, the key to success is turning to the right professional.

This guide will help you understand the role of a Certified Divorce Financial Analyst®, and how this financial neutral collaboration will help to enhance settlements.

I hope that you enjoy this book and I wish you great success in your family law practice.

Chapter 1:

The Institute for Divorce Financial Analysts™, and its certification

The main reason behind this book is because I am asked all the time to explain this title. While I am writing this, I am the only woman in my province to have the CDFA® title. While professionals with this certification will be saught after in the future, much information needs to be shared now.

To understand the financial certifications in Canada:

https://www.iiroc.ca/investors/UnderstandFinCert/Pages/default.aspx

For those of you in the United States, the different professional financial designations can be found here :

https://www.finra.org/investors/professional-designations

The rest of the book will be based on the Canadian certification and role.

The **Institute for Divorce Financial Analysis**, founded in 1993, certified more than 5,000 people as Certified Divorce Financial Analyst® professionals.

The institute was created to provide specialized training to professionals in these fields :

- Accounting
- Financial
- Matrimonial law

In order to obtain the certification, the individuals must follow a program, and have the required professional experience.

The program consists of two exams and the topics include :

- An overview of divorce law and family law
- Financial impact of divorce
- Analysing the financial data
- Matrimonial property law
- Financial expert in court
- Child/Spousal support

And many more .

In order to retain the certification , 15 hours of continuing education needs to be obtained every two years.

The profession of divorce financial planner is growing rapidly. Family Law practice firms are looking for ways to leverage their time, and individuals are becoming aware of this additional analysis and expertise.

The Institute for Divorce Financial Analysts have surveyed 276 CDFA® professionals and have released these statistics : (source DFA Journal Winter-Spring 2019)

- 79 % were in the Finance Industry
- 9% in accounting
- 6% in Law

And 63% are female.

Even though, in Canada, there are roughly 15% of Investment Advisors who are women, it is not surprising to see such a huge number of women as CDFA® professionals. There are still a lot of divorce cases where it is the woman who needs the help of a CDFA® professional.

Chapter 2 :
How a CDFA® professional contributes in your divorce cases.

A CDFA® professional in your team, or as an external consultant :

A) Analyses the financial issues of a separation and divorce.
B) Can interview clients and collect data.
C) Has knowledge of the legal and tax issues of a divorce
D) Can be an expert witness in your court proceeding.
E) Help develop a new budget, and a retirement objective
F) Identify if the current lifestyle can be kept or needs to be changed
G) Consolidate financial documents
H) Make an inventory of assets and uncover hidden revenues or assets
I) And much more

Financial Analysis

The financial analysis of the CDFA® professional will include :

i. When your client is fighting to keep the **matrimonial home**, an analysis is required to see if it is really the best solution. Can your client really keep up with the monthly payments, the taxes, the repairs ? Will there be enough cash flow to cover these? In a case where there is no revenu, but there is an investment account; the monthly withdrawals from that account will deplete the account over how many years ?

ii. **Pension plans**, retirement plans. They are all different. Some will be locked-in, some non-transferable until a certain date. A defined-benefit plan is different than a defined-contribution plan. The CDFA® professional will be able to explain to your client the difference between the defined-benefit vs defined-contribution pension plans. Some defined-benefits plans use the 'Best five-year average', and some the 'career average plan'.

Even though a pension valuation has to be done by an actuary (for the DB pension plan) , a CDFA® professional will help you make sense of it all.

iii. In the **division of assets**, the analysis must identify the short term and long-term effects. For example, one spouse gets the car, motorcycle, and RV, and the other spouse gets the rental property. It might be their wishes, (the spouse has an attachment to the vehicles) but it is not equitable down the road since the 3 will depreciate in value compared to the rental property which will appreciate.

iv. Evaluating **life insurance** needs. The spouse who receives spousal & child support should be named owner and beneficiary of the life insurance policy. As beneficiary, the spouse is sure to get the settlement in the case of death. And he/she is named as owner, so that the beneficiary designation cannot be changed along the way. The Payor of the policy (the person paying the monthly premium) is the person paying the spousal/child support. Where the person is no longer insurable, there are some options to look at.

v. Integrating **tax issues** into the proposed settlement. The assets being divided will have different tax implications. A simple example is the matrimonial home vs a cottage. Or a cash account vs a RSP or TFSA. A common mistake is looking at all the assets together as a bundle (example grouping all investment accounts together) and then trying to separate as one spouse keeps the cash account, and the other the RSP account. Each account has to be looked at separately.

vi. Analyze retirement plan issues, the pensions and retirement accounts. A CDFA® professional has a thorough knowledge of the different **retirement accounts**; RSP, RIF, LIRA, and LIF, and will be able to explain the contribution/withdrawal rules of each. Understanding the different withdrawal options at retirement and its tax implications is important to your client and his/her settlement. Furthermore, for younger clients, it will be important to discuss retirement planning and monthly contributions to a plan.

vii. Reviewing the **budget, income and expenses**. Working through the settlement process, each party will come up with their own budget & expenses. Revenues might be forgotten, and expenses might be counted twice. (Yearly expenses, like snow removal or taxes) . A common mistake is not checking what is included in the mortgage payment. The property taxes are included in the payment, and then counted again in housing expenses. Also, your client will need to make a brand new budget, based on the proposed settlement.

viii. **Assets, liabilities** and deemed costs of disposition. Each asset has to be analyzed separately. Consider the asset involved, the expected time of disposition, the fees & taxes of disposition, the Adjusted Cost Base. For example, a non-registered account (an account that is not a RSP or TFSA) is taxable, and you need to know the ACB to calculate its net after-tax value.

For the liabilities, each debt will have a different payment plan and interest rate.

ix. Review the current list of **deductions and exclusions**. Some spouses will try to exclude assets from the settlement. A common mistake amongst separating couples is thinking that a home owned by one before the marriage is excluded from the division of property. A property used as a family becomes part of the total property to be divided. *

*Each province has their own property statutes, and as a lawyer, it is your responsibility to make sure that your whole team is aware of it.

x. Identifying assets that were **disposed** of during the 2 years before the divorce proceedings. A spouse might have thought about divorcing for a while and had the opportunity and time to hide/liquidate assets.* Liquidating the assets in advance and 'preparing' towards a divorce does not work. The CDFA® professional will prepare a list of assets that were intentionally or recklessly depleted in the 2 previous years. A popular way of hiding assets is opening an account in the child's name .

*The 2-year window is an example. As a lawyer, advise your CDFA® professional about the time-frame of disposition in your jurisdiction.

xi. Can help your client understand that an **equitable division** of property does not always mean 50-50. Equitable and equal is not the same thing. The common argument is one spouse who has accumulated career assets does not want to divide them , because he/she has worked hard for that. Career assets include vacation pay, job experience, health club memberships, stock options, deferred bonuses, professional association dues, life/health/disability insurance, pension plans, etc.
As a lawyer, you will know whether the judges in your province consider career assets as part of property division.

xii. Examine the financial impact of a loss of **medical/dental coverage**. What one spouse pays under a group plan is not the same cost as an individual or family plan purchased outside a group plan. Also, it is important to check if your client is qualified to apply for a coverage with the same supplier within 90 days after the divorce. (a coverage applied without a medical questionnaire) . If your client cannot get a family medical/dental plan, a list of all the medical/dental expenses must be made. (the list should be prepared even if there is a plan, but even more important if there is none.)

Chapter 3

What a CDFA® Professional cannot do

A CDFA®professional will be a great asset to your Family Law Practice, either as an internal part of your group, or as an external consultant, but there are many things that cannot be delegated :

Legal Advice. Their role is to assist with the financial issues of a divorce, but not to replace you as the **lawyer** or **mediator**. Each spouse should seek separate legal counsel, unless it is an amicable separation and a mediator is used. The wordings that will be used in the analysis will be matter-of-fact, and no legal advice will be given.

Evaluations : A CDFA® professional is not an actuary, nor a Chartered Business Valuator. It is possible to have many titles but it is imporant to avoid any conflict of interest. A separation of duties is important.

An **actuary** will help with the valuation of a defined-benefit pension and statistically calculate life expectancies for insurance. For the pension valuations, you will want to make sure that the actuary used has experience and sufficient knowledge of pension values on marriage breakdown.

Chartered Business Valuator: If one or both spouses own a business, you will need to get it valued by a business valuator. If both spouses agree to the valuation of the business, it will be up to you to decide if the business valuator is necessary. (especially if the value quoted seems too high or too low, then you will want to explain the importance to your client)

Real Estate Appraiser: Similar to the business valuator, if both spouses agree to the same value, and it seems reasonable for the neighbourhood, maybe there is no need for the Real Estate Appraiser. A common mistake is where one spouse feels terrible about initiaing the divorce and will give in to the demands/quotes of the other spouse. It is important to do a thorough analysis of the assets and their market values, because once the divorce is finalised, the division of assets cannot be amended.

Doctor : in a case where one spouse has medical issues, only a doctor can determine his/her ability to work. In a disability case, where it can take months to get a decision or diagnosis, it would be prudent to wait for the official report.

A CDFA®professional will help you and your client understand the different benefits available , including Employment Insurance Disability Insurance (15 weeks maximum) , CPP disability benefits (up to age 65), and also from their work group's insurance : short-term and long-term coverage.

Human resources person:

Even though a CDFA® professional understands and can explain employee benefit programs, stock options, retirement plans and packages , you might want to ask for a meeting with the spouse's employer' human resources person. Because each company is different, go straight to the source, and save time and money.

A CPA, accountant, tax preparer. Even though the CDFA® professional will help you with the tax issues related to the divorce, it would be a conflict of interest for a CDFA® professional to prepare income tax returns for your client, even if they have both titles of CDFA® and CPA.

Chapter 4

Delegate the financial analysis tasks to grow your practice.

I am a strong believer that to succeed in business, you have to surround yourself with amazing people, other professionals and be open to collaboration.

Spend as much time as possible doing what you are good in, and delegate the rest. (well, I also mean spend your working hours growing your business by doing what you are trained at doing)

In a divorce case, you are confronted with the legal aspects, the emotional roller coaster of your client and sometimes complex financial situations with tremendous wealth.

Some cases are complicated by verbal/physical/emotional abuse, parental alienation, child protection services, bankruptcy, depression, etc, and since you should spend your time working on the legal aspects, why not delegate the financial aspect to an expert?

I have been in the financial industry for 15 years and I have met a lot of lawyers (through networking and meetings). Most admitted that family law is a cut-throat business, and that many lawyers make much less money than we think. Look around ,the ones that succeed are the ones who collaborate with other professionals.

In your family law practice, you might have a lot of cases where it is straightforward, the exes just want to get this divorce over with. There is an amicable understanding that the best must be done for the sake of the children.

Then, there is that case, where the exes are bitter. There is fighting over everything, including custody of the kids & the dogs, and who gets the expensive stereo system and art collection. Even this case you can handle, you have seen it many times.

However, there are some cases where you will want to win, at all cost, because your client is going through something so difficult, so unjust, that you will want to connect with a CDFA® professional.

This is the type of case that I get asked to work with :

- The ex-husband has a company
- Declares little revenu
- Mixes up personal/business expenses
- Multiple bank accounts in Canada and USA
- Several credit cards
- Seems to have investment accounts (because he declares interest, dividends and capital gains.)
- Understands really well the income tax rules

Since child support is based on revenues, and not total assets or wealth, your client (who has a regular job and salary), might end up paying him child support. Many people going through this are asking why does this happen ?

You know why. Lack of time, resources and money. (not your money, the client's money) You charge per hour. And you know that this type of analysis (reviewing all of the financial documents) would be around 200 hours.

You cannot charge, let's say, $200 per hour for 200 hours, to review financial documents to try to prove that the ex-husband makes more money than he declares.

One of the most important tasks that you will delegate to your CDFA® professional will be the collection of data. The data will then be used in the evaluation and analysis of the income, deductions, budget, assets and liablilities of your clients.

The financial information has to be as accurate as possible, because this is used for the negocation between the spouses and their lawyers.

The following pages describe the collection and review of the financial data .

Data
collection

The CDFA® professional will ask for the following documents:

- For business owners : Financial statements for the past 3 years. Balance sheet, income statement, cash flow statement, and statement of shareholders' equity.
- Income tax returns for the past 3 years
- List of investment accounts with pertinent details
- Employee benefit booklet and current option choices (medical/dental/ and insurance coverage chosen within the group plan)
- Information about the mortgage(s)
- The last 3 paystubs
- List of assets
- List of debts

- Marital property inventory
- Property inventory to be excluded
- Household inventory
- Current budget
- Bank account statements
- Credit card statements
- Credit report
- Child and spousal support (paid or received , from a previous relationship)
- Life, Critical Illness and Disability insurance information
- Other documents that have an impact on the financial situation.

This first step of data collection can take a while, and there will be a lot of back-and-forth with the clients to get all of the documents required. The CDFA® professional will keep you updated on the collection of these documents.

Reviewing the data collected

The CDFA® professional will go through the financial data, look for double-counting, discrepancies and oddities.

Here are some examples of questionable items:

- Income tax returns given without the official Notice of Assessment; there is no way of knowing if it is what was really submitted to the government.
- Every 'other' item should be explained, for example 'other household expense'
- High amounts for grocery bills and restaurants. If the amounts seem high, ask for receipts.

- Gifts : Birthday gifts are often counted twice as shoes and clothing. If the gift item seems high, ask for details.
- Car costs. Some will forget to add maintenance costs/ winter-tire change, or this number can be exagerrated.
- Medical/dental expenses in the budget does not correspond to what is in the Income Tax return Or for a spouse who will be left without a group Insurance; he/she might forget to add this expense in the new budget.

- Valuation date of assets and debts. Make sure your clients both use the same marriage/valuation date. This might seem obvious, but I have seen a case where the husband gave the wrong date of marriage and this was used in the court documents. The valuation date varies by province (most use the date of separation).
- Market values : family antiques should be appraised by a professional and all of the furniture should be itemised using garage-sale prices (not purchase price)

- Non-registered accounts must show the adjusted cost base . If this amount (ACB) seems low, ask for an Unrealised capital gain/loss report. This report , from the Invesment Firm, will show the ACB and invested capital.
- Disposition costs. Some investments have deferred sales charges, fees and /or commissions if sold.

There are many more examples that could be given. What is important to remember is that the CDFA® professional is used to reviewing these numbers and will let you know if more information is required.

Further inquiries

Most of your cases will probably go as planned, where the documents are requested, received and analysed without any problems.

In the case where one spouse has a business and seems to hide assets and revenues, the CDFA® professional might request further documents.

Here are some things that might be questioned:

- **Business expenses*** : expenses are deducted from the revenues, to pay as little taxes as possible. Soft-expenses, like home office, cell phone, vehicule and 'miscellaneous' are normally added back.

- **Financial fees*:** these give you a clue as to the market value of the person's Investment Portfolio. Portfolio Managers have different ways of charging fees. One way is a flat-fee of 1%, for example. Financial fees for RSP and TFSA are not tax-deductible. Thus if the client is showing a financial fee of $10,000, it might represent a million-dollar portfolio.
- **Interest fees*:** you can deduct interest fees paid in order to invest. (not interest payments on credit cards) So if this amount is high, it might represent , again, an investment asset.

(* verify with your taxation specialist)

- **Interest, dividends, and capital gains** (losses) in an income tax return shows that the person has investments. A review of the tax slips indicate the type of account, and at which institution.
- Income tax **deductions.** Deductions are used to decrease as much as possible the net income (thus to pay less taxes). A clarification (proof) of those deductions my be requested.
- Copies of deposited/cancelled **cheques** could be required. This is obtained by the bank. The reason is to question expenses. A business owner could write a false cheque to an accountant, make a photocopy, but then destroy the cheque.

- Subpeona **bank/ investment accounts**. The real income cannot be established unless all of the account statements are received. Since the person might want to take their time or hide assets/revenues, it is better to send subpeonas. The analysis will include every deposit/withdrawal/ transfer and expense.
- Credit/account **statements** might reveal a few things themselves. For example, monthly trips to the Pharmacy with similar amounts, but yet the medical expenses deduction in the income tax return does not match. Not declaring medical expenses is a way to appear poor (you do not have money to go to the dentist or go to the chiro) .

Thus requesting information from the pharmacy, dentist and chiro might reveal a larger lifestyle.

- **Large payments received/paid.** Exact amounts that repeat every month should be questioned. For example, a client who is trying to hide the co-ownership of a duplex. There is a monthly rent payment (because the person declared to be renting) along with another amount that looks like a mortgage payment.

Chapter 5:

For mediators; how a CDFA® can help with the negotiations*

*the following information is about mediators in Quebec, Canada

A mediator helps the divorcing couple reach a fair agreement on the subjects discussed during meditation.

The subjects normally include:

- Child custody
- Child support
- Spousal support
- Division of property

Mediation is voluntary and either spouse can refuse to participate or end at any time. If there is no collaboration, or either spouse refuses to work with the mediator, the next step would be to consult a lawyer.

A mediator is not a psychologist, nor a therapist, nor to be used to save a marriage.

The mediator cannot :

- Make decisions for the couple, (only a judge can make decisions)
- Represent only one spouse, or take one side
- Give legal opinions

Mediation is done in three parts.

1) Evaluation of the situation
2) Negociation on points that were raised .
3) Creating the report on points agreed on.

The CDFA® professional will be an asset during the evaluation of the couple's situation and is trained to work with clients from different financial backgrounds :

- One spouse earns the most
- The two spouses both earn similar salaries
- A retired couple
- One spouse is retired but one is still working

During the evaluation and negotiation stages, the mediator will ensure that both parents communicate their needs and expectations freely.

Contrary to what happens in the courtroom, mediation is a collaboration, and the two separating spouses have better control over the decisions.

There will be some situations where one spouse does not have a grasp of reality, and the CDFA® professional will help you manage client's expectations.

Case study:

- Couple separating after a 20-year marriage
- Three kids in college and University
- Wife never worked but has a post-secondary diploma
- She is 48 yrs old and is healthy
- He has a salary of $86,000 a year
- They were able to survive financially, but never saved any money.
- She thinks he will continue to pay for her for the rest of her life, since it is his fault they are divorcing.
- Mediation negocations were not getting anywhere because of her lack of understanding

While the mediator was able to explain the no-fault-divorce, the CDFA® professional helped with making the client understand the limitation of an $86,000 yearly salary.

The steps taken with her were:

- Creating a new budget for him and her
- Looking at the annual income and expenses
- Reviewing the current housing costs for either a home purchase or rental.
- Explaining the disposable income VS earned gross income.

The female client had never paid a bill in the 20-year marriage. It was an eye-opener once she worked on the new budget and all of the yearly expenses were in the Excel sheet (Christmas gifts, car license, birthday gifts, etc.)

Once the net income, expenses and overall yearly budget was reviewed, she learned that the $86,000 gross salary meant an after-tax income of $62,265 * ($5188.75 monthly). In her head, $86,000 gross meant a $7500 monthly income.

She agreed to start looking for a job and getting on with her life. At the end, making sure that the children's education was paid for was more important to her.

* https://www.ey.com/ca/en/services/tax/tax-calculators-2019-personal-tax

Chapter 6:

Effectively use a CDFA® as an Expert witness

In your Family Law practice, you might want to use as many expert witnesses as possible to prove your case. In the case of a CDFA® professional ,he/she will be able to give an expert opinion, interpretation and analysis on the financial documents provided by the other team.

An expert witness is used to assist the judge in determining and understanding specific evidence. The CDFA® professional must have the knowledge, skill, training and education to testify.

When chosing to work with CDFA® professionals, these are some questions you could ask :

- How long they have been practicing in their career ?
- Since when do they have the CDFA® title ?
- What type of case do they normally work with?
- Do they work with individuals themselves or only with lawyers/mediators ?
- Did they have any lawsuits ?
- Was their professional license ever suspended ?
- Were they ever fired from a position?
- Could they be an expert witness ?
- Could they take the questionning from the other lawyer ?
- Is their résumé up to date ?

Verfication of their qualification :

For the CDFA® title, this certification can be checked on the IDFA website :
https://institutedfa.com/

For the CDFA® professionals who are Investment Advisors, you can check their registration with IIROC (in Canada) :

https://www.iiroc.ca/investors/knowyouradvisor/Pages/default.aspx

or in USA :
https://www.adviserinfo.sec.gov/IAPD/Default.aspx

Verification of any complaints & lawsuits.

Since verifying their registration is only half of it, you should also check if there are any complaints & lawsuits filed against them

For Canada :

https://www.iiroc.ca/industry/enforcement/Pages/Search-Disciplinary-Cases.aspx

and USA :

https://www.sec.gov/litigations/sec-action-look-up

Tips :

Depending where you have your Family law practice, you might want to think about these before starting to meet CDFA® professionals or their résumés.

- Do you need the person to be bilingual ? (English-Spanish, English-French) etc. ..
- Do you have time to help them get prepared for court ? If not, you will want a highly experienced CDFA® with court appearances.
- Would you rather they have a law or financial background ?
- Are the other firms in your area hiring CDFA® professionals, or it is new ? If it is new, be prepared to explain to the courts what is a CDFA® professional.

- What is the compensation plan ? Salaried, hourly ?
- Do you need more than one to satisfy all of your demands ?
- Etc. Think about your needs before you start interviewing.

Cross Examination

The CDFA® might not have a lot of experience as an expert witness. He/she must be made aware that being an expert witness is not as simple as dictating your analysis on the stand. The lawyer from the opposing team will try to discredit the person and analysis, however, the process will be more pleasant if your witness is prepared for trial.

Here are some tips to share with your CDFA®: (as a lawyer, you already know this, but do not assume that your CDFA® does)

- Always be truthful (if you do not know the answer- say so.)
- Listen carefully to the entirety of the question. And if it is not clear, say so.
- Only answer the questions asked, with a 'yes' or 'no'. If you try to elaborate, or explain, you will look defensive. Let your lawyer rephrase the question or ask you to explain.
- Take your time to think about your answer.
- Be self-assured, do not be forced into giving an answer.
- Keep your emotions in check. Any attitude or fighting makes you lose credibility.
- Try to relax, you are probably the only one in the room who truly understands all of this finance stuff.

Chapter 7: Find a CDFA® that matches your firm's vision

You can find a CDFA® professional in your area by searching on the IDFA's website. At the same time, you will know if the person's certification is still valid.

https://institutedfa.com/find-a-cdfa/

Finding someone in your area is important, but even more important is finding someone who shares the same vision and ethical values as you and your team.

It could be detrimental to your firm's reputation if you refer your clients to someone who lacks professionalism, ethics and even kindness……

Your firm's vision

If your Family Law Practice is newly up and running, you had to ask yourself what is the mission and vision of your firm.

After the first year, you can look back and see if it still fits. Over the years, your practice will have evolved and you will see if this vision statement is still aligned with your brand.

The CDFA® that you hire as an internal or external consultant has to fit your vision statement.

Ethical Values

What ethical values are important to you and your firm ? Here are some examples of Core Ethical Values :

- Trustworthiness: Does this person seem loyal, truthful, sincere ?
- Respect: Will this person respect your firm and the clients?
- Responsibility : Does this person show a sense of responsibility and accountability ?
- Fairness: Can this person show fairness and impartiality ?
- Kindness: Does this person seem kind, caring and compassionate ?

Conflict of interest

During the divorce process, you cannot use the CDFA® for multiple roles. For example, a tax specialist cannot do your client's income taxes and be the CDFA® who analyses the divorce case.

Summary

A CDFA® professional can be an added asset to your family law practice. Since you can delegate the financial analysis of your divorce cases, it liberates precious time to concentrate on the rest of your case.

They cannot give legal advice, but they serve as :

A litigation support

Financial Expert

Data Collector

Budget & cash flow preparer

Manager of client expectations

Expert witness in court proceedings

www.ingramcontent.com/pod-product-compliance
Lightning Source LLC
Chambersburg PA
CBHW060408080526
44583CB00012B/509